thank you: a little book of
gratitude

thank you: a little book of

gratitude

how saying thanks can
change your life

lois blyth

CICO BOOKS

LONDON NEW YORK

Published in 2022 by CICO Books
An imprint of Ryland Peters & Small Ltd

20–21 Jockey's Fields   341 E 116th St
London WC1R 4BW   New York, NY 10029

www.rylandpeters.com

10 9 8 7 6 5 4 3 2 1

Text © Sarah Sutton 2017
Design and illustration © CICO Books 2022

A CIP catalog record for this book is available from
the Library of Congress and the British Library.

ISBN: 978-1-80065-168-5

Printed in China

Commissioning editor: Kristine Pidkameny
Publishing manager: Carmel Edmonds
Editors: Rosie Lewis and Slav Todorov
Designers: Geoff Borin and Fahema Khanam
Illustrator: Daniel Haskett
Art director: Sally Powell
Creative director: Leslie Harrington
Production manager: Gordana Simakovic

Contents

Introduction

Whole-hearted gratitude is an uplifting, expansive, and positive way of being that leads to appreciation and times of fun and laughter. Sharing, caring, and togetherness are some of the essentials of being human. Feeling thankful makes us want to give back—to those who have helped us, cared for us, who love us—or who quite simply make us happy.

The magic happens when thoughts of gratitude are transformed into positive action. They become a gift of wholehearted appreciation that expands with further giving. Each time one person expresses gratitude to another, the feeling of being appreciated encourages both people to be more generous-spirited to others—and so it goes on.

Using this book

This book doesn't need to be read from cover to cover. It is designed to be dipped into—for reassurance, to help you regain perspective, or to prompt ideas for gifts or giving. It can be used as a source of daily wisdom or as an occasional guide.

"*Nothing is more honorable than the grateful heart.*"

Seneca (4 BCE–36 CE), Roman philosopher

"When you rise in the morning, give thanks for the light, for your life, for your strength. Give thanks for your food and for the joy of living. If you see no reason to give thanks, the fault lies in yourself."

Tecumseh (1768–1813), Shawnee Chief

CHAPTER 1

getting started

Saying "thank you" is common courtesy in every language—
we all use this expression of gratitude everyday. It is more
than a polite habit of speech. When we focus on increasing
our level of appreciation, we bring greater joy and
enrichment to our lives. The intention throughout this book is
not to overwhelm you with things to do and rituals to keep
to, but simply to invite you to dip in with an open mind to the
possibilities that living with gratitude can offer.

Start Where You Are

Gratitude is not a destination; it is a state of mind and being.

You can quite simply start where you are, right now,
with three simple questions:

Who do I feel grateful to have in my life?

What has already happened today I can be thankful for?

How shall I record this moment or show my appreciation?

Making a habit of answering these questions can quickly make
your life happier and more contented. You will learn more about
how to answer these questions in the pages that follow.

Nurturing Gratitude

Gratitude, like all newly planted seeds, needs patience, warmth, and nurture to allow it to grow and to give it the space and time to shine. It may be sensitive in the early stages of growth and easily suffocated by darker feelings of bitterness, anger, resentment, and jealousy, which absorb too much energy. By staying attentive and weeding out unhelpful attitudes, you can allow gratitude and thankfulness to burgeon.

Companionship, friendship, shared laughter, and kindness help gratitude to develop unabated. Regular feeding with appreciation, understanding, and courtesy also works wonders. But beware of doubt, suspicion, and cynicism; they are common pests that undermine sincerity. The moment any kind of ulterior motive is suspected, genuine thankfulness falters and finds it harder to thrive.

With regular nurture, gratitude will flower into optimism and positivity that sustain health and well-being for life.

Gratitude in Practice

Living life with conscious gratitude

In her book *Fragile Mystics* (2015), Rev. Magdalen Smith introduces us to Rosie Pinto de Carvalho, who tells her: "I don't have everything I love, but I love everything I have." Rosie lives in a favela in one of the poorest areas of Rio de Janeiro, Brazil. What an inspiring attitude to life! In that single comment, Rosie reinforces awareness that there is very little connection between material possessions and contentment. The less we own, the more we appreciate and treasure what our belongings represent.

Starting a Gratitude Journal

An attitude of gratitude gains strength the more we practice it.

Making simple changes to the way we view the world each day gradually adjusts our perspective, almost without us noticing. So this section is all about you—and for you. It begins with a carefully chosen gift to yourself: your gratitude journal, app, or diary.

Give your choice of journal some thought before you embark on your mission of gratitude, because it needs to become a joy to use. I was very lucky that a dear friend had given me a beautiful notebook that had been waiting two years for the right moment to be used.

It was exactly the right size, shape, and quality to inspire me—but I am an old-fashioned pen-and-paper person. If you are likely to share some key moments on Twitter or Pinterest, you may prefer to use your cell phone or a specially designed app to record your moments of gratitude.

"Preserve your memories, keep them well."

Louisa May Alcott (1832–1888), writer

Why Keep a Gratitude Journal?

You may find yourself feeling skeptical about starting a gratitude journal. "What is the point? What a cliché. What good will it do? I haven't got time…" There are many reasons why we might tell ourselves that there is no point in giving the process a try. If you find yourself feeling resistant to the idea, perhaps pause to ask yourself:

What have I got to lose?

As someone who was initially doubtful that my journal would be much more than a list of "thank yous," I was amazed at how quickly and how profoundly the process affected the way I viewed my experiences. Because the journal is intended only for positive thoughts, it forces the writer to find a way to reframe everyday happenings. The scientists are right. By deliberately choosing a positive outlook we do gradually alter the way we think—about ourselves and about the events that happen to us and around us.

The Six As of Thankfulness

Choose your **Attitude**—Finding ways to develop
a consciously positive outlook is an integral part
of becoming "thank full."

Increase **Awareness**—Tuning in to your environment
and the events of each day increases consciousness.

Appreciate the everyday—Finding joy in small things
expands our appreciation of the bigger things, too.

Allocate time—If you are writing a journal, it can be
helpful to do it at the same time each day, so that you
begin to remember automatically.

Remain **Authentic**—Everyone has their own style of
behavior and of expression. Stay true to yourself.

Acceptance—The most important "A" of all. Gratitude
is at its most powerful when you allow others to give,
and can accept wholeheartedly.

What Should I Write About?

Now you have a gratitude journal, what should you write about? The easy answer is anything and everything—or anyone—that holds meaning for you and has an impact on your life, whether now or in the past. You might feel thankful for something that you have experienced personally, or grateful for something that has happened to someone else. It could be something as simple as hearing a great new track on the radio or buying a new sweater, or as profound as being reunited with a friend, or hearing news of a neighbor who is recovering from illness.

People: your friends, family, neighbors, colleagues, kind strangers, teachers, past acquaintances, anyone who has inspired you.

Places: home and what it means to you, vacation places that trigger wonderful memories, places of interest that inspire you, destinations that feed your imagination and dreams for the future.

Heritage: where you came from, your culture, traditions, and history.

Things: wonderful objects, clever design, amazing architecture: the joy of driving your car, enjoying a great movie or TV series, the comfort of your favorite chair after spending time away.

The natural world: the sky, sea, animals, birds, trees, plants, the weather, and landscape offer so much that inspires us and that we can be grateful for.

You: your uniqueness, your talents, foibles, friends, successes and failures, goals and achievements.

Changing Perspective

Oprah Winfrey is well known for her actively positive attitude to life, and she has spoken about the importance of her gratitude journal.

Interestingly, she has also written about the impact of being too busy to keep up her journal. After a particularly busy period when she was feeling less joy in her work, she took time to look back at a journal entry from a year or two earlier and noticed how much more contented she had been then. She realized on reflection that she had been no less busy during that year—she had simply been more disciplined about making time to reflect each day on the good things that had happened. When she took time to look for reasons to feel grateful, "something always showed up."

Martin Seligman (see page 53) recommends thinking of "three good things" about each day. He has proven that this simple action leads directly to an increase in well-being. You could try it for yourself. It is as simple as:

1. _____

2. _____

3. _____

As you develop the gratitude habit, you will discover that you go to greater depths with your thoughts. You may want to write more expressively about what the pathway to gratitude has shown you—and how it is transforming your thinking.

1. It was lovely of Jo to insist on picking me up when my car broke down earlier.

2. If I hadn't broken down I wouldn't have had the chance to spend so much time chatting with her and her daughter.

3. I am so relieved that the car broke down today and not on the way to work on Monday. It is interesting how often something good comes out of something annoying.

How Reframing Works in Practice

Looking on the bright side

"Although I am terrified by the idea of the medical treatment, I am hugely relieved that I now know what is wrong with me—and the medical team are being wonderful. I am starting to allow myself to hope that I can get through this."

Being completely honest with yourself

"Although I am devastated that I have been made redundant, and I am still very worried about the future, I must admit that I had been thinking of leaving that job for a while, and perhaps this period may give me time to retrain."

Acknowledging the dark side

"Although this is a disruptive time, I feel grateful for the memory of the arguments we had because it helps me to know in my heart that it is better that we have parted."

Gratitude in Practice

The bigger picture

"I had become fed up with certain aspects of my job," says Grace, "and was thinking of leaving. I was having trouble thinking of anything positive to write in my gratitude journal, too, so I flicked back through it, partly for inspiration. I came across a couple of entries that described how grateful felt to get the job in the first place! That helped me to think about the bigger picture and things I can do to bring about changes in my place of work instead, rather than leaving and causing upheaval."

Creating a Sacred Space

Is there an area in your home where you can feel at peace? For some it will be a whole room; for others it may be a particular chair, or a spot by a window or outside in the garden.

This can become a sacred space for contemplation. If you feel anxious about the sense of ritual involved, be reassured that there is no need for any kind of faith or conscious belief for this process to be helpful. Making space within your world for a positive nook that you automatically associate with feelings of wholehearted thanks can trigger wonderful feelings of peace and acceptance.

A sense of calm is essential for replenishing feelings of gratitude, especially after a taxing or tiring day. Creating an area for contemplation can help you to feel more connected, focused, and grounded. Just as you would clear your work surfaces before preparing to cook or create something, so too it makes sense to clear your mind before focusing on all there is to feel grateful for.

Creating a Gratitude Altar

Altars have played an important part in rites and rituals of thanksgiving since prehistoric times, as well as being an anchor point for receiving the sacrament in Western religions. Creating an altar is very personal. If you feel moved to make one in your home, think about whether you want it to be in a place that is light and bright in the morning, or cozy and softly lit for use in the evenings. Do you want to be able to hear sounds of birdsong outside your window, or do you want silence or music so that you can shut out the world? You may like to include:

- Candles—scented or unscented

- Flowers

- Natural elements, such as pebbles, shells, and/or leaves

- Symbols that have personal meaning for you, such as a ring, crystals, or a sacred object

Grateful Meditation

Allow your body to relax, from your toes to the top of your head.

Pay special attention to letting go of the tension in different areas of your body, such as your feet, knees, shoulders, or jawline, by stretching, moving your body, or even yawning.

Be aware of whether you are starting from a mood of anger, frustration, or sadness—or whether you are already feeling positive and full of gratitude. Don't judge yourself for your feelings, or try to change them; just be aware of your state of mind.

Now breathe easily and naturally. Be patient with yourself, and begin to observe and recollect. Consider whom or what you are thankful for, and why.

Depending on your state of mind, it may help to focus on a few details:

- The dawn chorus that I heard this morning.

- My warm gratitude toward the young boy who helped me yesterday.

- The bright yellow of the daffodils that are coming into flower.

- The amazing full moon in such a beautifully clear sky the other evening.

Simply noticing and appreciating the positive elements of the world around you will have an uplifting effect. Starting off with small things leads quickly to thoughts of the big things:

- The love of my family.

- The kindness of my friends.

- The joy of watching my team score at the weekend.

- My relative health and the use of my body.

- The financial security that my job offers me.

- The memory of my mother's light and wisdom.

If you become distracted, watch where your attention goes. Don't fight your thoughts, but see whether you can reframe them with gratitude. For example, if someone has been annoying you: "I am grateful for having X as my friend, even though he has been driving me insane lately. I know he has been going through a hard time. I will give him a call."

"*Let us be thankful to people who make us happy; they are the gardeners who make us blossom.*"

Marcel Proust (1871–1922), writer

CHAPTER 2

gratitude is good for us

Scientific research is gradually building a body of evidence
that supports what we have always known instinctively—that
gratitude is good for our health. It shows up not only in the
way we look after our physical fitness and nutritional health,
but also in our mental well-being and lifestyle choices.
Gratitude helps us to develop an optimistic outlook and plays
an important role in how we feel about our life, work,
and purpose.

The Healing Power
of Gratitude

In 2015, the *Journal of Happiness Studies* (yes, there really is such a publication!) reported on a short-term study in the United States that compared the benefits to patients of keeping a) a gratitude journal; b) a kindness journal; and c) no journal over a period of 14 days, while they were waiting to be referred to a counselor. Interestingly, the only group that felt any benefit during such a short period of time was the one that focused on gratitude.

What Does a Grateful Brain Look Like?

Researchers have found that when people express gratitude, their brains show increased levels of activity in the anterior cingulate cortex and the medial prefrontal cortex. Both areas are associated with the way we process emotions and express empathy, our bonds with others, and moral judgment.

Choose Your Words
With Care

The enemies of gratitude are negative thoughts, which influence
our choice of words and then our actions. Pay attention to how you
react and the words you use when faced with disappointment, or
when things don't quite go to plan. Our use of language tells us
a great deal about our state of mind: "I wish," "I regret," "If only,"
"I should have," "I wanted to," "I am fed up," "Why should I,"
"I can't ... "

Oh, the joy of "shoulda, woulda, coulda." All these phrases are
energy depleters that take away our personal power and deplete
our positivity. Over time, as we blame other people or bad luck
for our circumstances, we begin to feel powerless over our own
lives. It may become harder to feel joy or to act spontaneously,
and difficult to forgive those around us for being less than perfect,
or the world for not living up to our expectations. The natural power
of gratitude, however, is such that it is also quite easy to adjust our
responses and reframe our experience in a more positive light,
if we choose to do so.

Try thinking to yourself, or writing down, or saying
out loud in a private moment each day:

I am thankful for...

I am grateful for...

I appreciate...

I am glad that...

I offer gratitude for...

How kind that...

gratitude guru: **Eleanor H. Porter**

The original gratitude guru must be Pollyanna, a fictional character in the American classic children's story of the same name by Eleanor H. Porter. Unfailingly (and, some would say, unrelentingly) positive and cheery, Pollyanna is taught by her father to look for the good in everything and to be "glad" for every obstacle she faces in life, because something positive will be revealed in every situation.

> *"There is something about everything that you can be glad about, if you keep hunting long enough to find it."*

Eleanor H. Porter (1868–1920), *Pollyanna*

The Pollyanna Factor

On a scale of 1 to 10, what is your Pollyanna-style "Gladness" score?

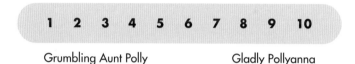

1   2   3   4   5   6   7   8   9   10

Grumbling Aunt Polly   Gladly Pollyanna

Are you somewhere between 5 and 10? Are you Pollyanna—a fully paid-up optimist, glad to be alive and grateful for everything that happens to you? Do you more often find yourself at the lower end of the scale—more Aunt Polly than Pollyanna? (See also the quiz on pages 134–135.) Most of us are in the middle, around 5 or 6: full of enthusiasm one minute and easily let down the next; programmed to believe that everything will get better, but not beyond moaning a great deal when things don't work out as planned.

The ABC of Optimism

If we want to alter the way we react to situations and become more grateful, we must consciously change the way we think before and during an event or occurrence. Think about it as the **A, B, C** of optimism:

A is the trigger for the negative thoughts.

B is the behavior that has become an automatic response to that thought.

C is the consequence.

For example:

Each time your friend turns up late (A—the trigger) you start to feel resentment (B—the behavior). Rather than saying how you really feel, you say something sarcastic, which leads to an argument—which somehow turns out to be your fault (C—the consequence). If, however, you know that her lateness will lead to you feeling resentful, you can be on the alert before A takes place, and prepare an alternative strategy.

For example, you could say: "Shall we meet an hour later, as I know you find it hard to get here promptly from work?" Or, if you are feeling braver, "I need to let you know that when you turn up late every time, I take it personally."

The Role of Patience

The ability to delay gratification in childhood has long been associated with a greater capacity for material success in later life. However, factors that are allied with this are patience and gratitude. In a study in the United States, participants were given the choice between receiving an immediate cash reward or waiting up to 12 months for a larger windfall of as much as $100. It turned out that those who showed the least patience and gratitude tended to claim payment at the $18 mark. The more grateful people held out, on average, until the amount reached $30. The conclusion was that when we feel thankful for what we already have, we are less likely to be impatient in our responses and give in to the impulse for immediate gratification. (This sounds like a conclusion that is good for relationships, too!)

When Gratitude Doesn't Work

There is one negative trait that can become associated with the habit of gratitude: some people have the potential to develop a false sense of reality. This can take the form of an extreme and rather fatalistic belief that life is so positive that everything will be okay, whatever the evidence to the contrary. This can lead to problems such as ignoring bills, not going to the doctor, not acknowledging that something needs to be repaired. Gratitude does not absolve us from responsibility; it is more about achieving balance—appreciating that life is about giving and receiving rather than expecting and taking.

Gratitude in Practice

Taking time to feel grateful

"I became very interested in practicing positivity in a conscious way after a particularly difficult time in my life," says Gina. "I have been told that I am a bit of an 'Eeyore' in my approach to things, and I worry a great deal. I wanted to see whether consciously changing my thoughts would make a permanent difference. However, after an enthusiastic beginning I found that I began to feel guilty if I did not feel grateful straight away. Many of the self-help books made me feel worse instead of better—as if I was doing something wrong. Living with gratitude is not a simple matter of saying that 'the world is alright' and then it shall be so. Some serious work has to be done along the way to consciously change one's thoughts and approach. These days I take my time to feel grateful. I aim to reframe things in a more positive light."

Be Grateful for Your Body

How many hours, days, or weeks have we all spent regretting that our bodies have some perceived flaw? The physical frame that you call a body carries you, enables you to breathe, and keeps your heart beating, even—within limits—when it is mistreated with the wrong kind of food, unhealthy behavior, or negative thoughts. It may be time to show gratitude for your physical self by giving your body more of what it really needs to flourish and maintain good health. Take the pledge to give thanks for your body every day! List three things that you like about your body and would like to give thanks for.

Remember:

1. One note of appreciation

2. One observation

3. One deeper thought

Conscious Nourishment

- Feel grateful for the foods you enjoy that are healthy,
and eat more of them.

- Feel thankful that sometimes, when we think we are
hungry, we are simply bored, anxious, or thirsty.

- Feel delighted that our bodies prefer to heal and get well
if they can. If you focus on swapping unhealthy patterns for
healthy ones, it will get easier to maintain your new lifestyle.

- Finally, "think gratitude" for your new plan of action when you go
shopping for food. That way, you will be less likely to
overspend or to buy food that is less nourishing and that
you will feel less grateful for later.

Give Back to Your Body

If you have been neglecting exercise and need to get started again, you may like to consider one or more of the following to begin with:

- Go for a meaningful walk each day—around the block, to a nearby park, or to somewhere new.

- Music is one of the most incredible gifts of all. Our bodies are designed for movement, so who can resist getting up to dance when the sound matches our mood? Dancing is exercise and pure enjoyment rolled into one.

- Treat yourself to an occasional massage or reflexology session. In the right hands a treatment will help to balance your body and get rid of tension, so that your blood flows more readily, your gut works more healthily, and you feel revitalized.

- If you have access to a garden, spending 20 minutes or so a day weeding, planting, and nurturing will reap great rewards—for you as well as the plants.

- If you feel more adventurous, offering gratitude to others by taking part in a sponsored walk, half-marathon, or other challenge for a greater cause can help to get you focused, motivated, and fit at the same time.

Making Time for Gratitude

We all lead busy lives, so "making time" for additional activities is not always an option. The beauty of living life more thankfully is that small changes in everyday thoughts and outlook can reap big rewards—with no need to find "extra" time in your daily routine.

"A grateful heart is a magnet for miracles."

Anonymous

"People may forget what you said or forget what you did, but they will never forget how you made them feel."

Anonymous

CHAPTER 3

giving, receiving, and reciprocating

Gratitude is a dance of give and take (literally), and the gift lies as much in the joy of giving as in the pleasure of receiving—and sometimes more so. For acceptance is in itself a gift, and a precious one at that. Giving, receiving, and reciprocating lie at the heart of families, communities, and the civilized world as we know it. When we share, we all thrive and survive—and we develop a sense of care and belonging. Receiving a gift that has meaning tells us that we have been recognized and accepted for who we are. A thank you offered with heart is also a gift of love and appreciation. When we give rather than take, the whole world feels like a better and more generous place to be.

Giving

Gratitude is associated with giving and with whole-hearted appreciation in all its various forms. When we think about gratitude, we relate it to a wish to appreciate and celebrate, but at its core, giving is about sharing and reaching out to others. The word comes from the Latin word *gratia*, meaning grace, graciousness, or gratefulness. It is not only a feeling—it can also become a state of being.

Choosing a Gift

When we put time aside to focus on someone who holds
meaning for us, we begin to reflect on ourselves, too:

- Would she like this?

- Does he have one?

- If I get it wrong, will he/she think I don't care?

- Will he want one?

- Why don't I know more about his/her taste?

- Will it suit her?

As adults, we find it easier to give than to receive, so it is important
to respect one another's needs, and to consider our wish to give
from the receiver's perspective as well as our own.

Who is Giving to Whom?

Gift-giving has a way of becoming stressful when it becomes more about personal need than the wish to honor someone else. Perhaps...

- the giver becomes so concerned about causing disappointment that they can no longer trust his or her own judgment to choose;

- in an effort to please, and in fear of being judged, the giver spends more money than he or she can afford;

- the receiver is more focused on his or her own needs and wants than on the care the giver has taken.

The greatest gifts are not material gifts at all. They are expressed through the real time we choose to spend with one another, the genuine acknowledgment that we offer for things that are done for us, and our voiced recognition of the time, effort, and care involved in those loving gifts. There is a time-honored rhythm to gratitude. It is a three-step waltz of giving, receiving, and reciprocating.

Keeping Things Special

Children, especially, look forward each year to birthday celebrations, festivities, and times of giving with enormous hope and excitement. Seeing a child's face as they receive and unwrap a gift is a precious treat in itself. No wonder so many parents and grandparents buy more and more lavish gifts to enjoy the reward of an excited child's grateful smile. But gifts lose their glister when we receive them too often. Expectations become greater and the magic of receiving diminishes, because it is no longer rare or special. It's the gift equivalent of your favorite song being played endlessly on the radio, or the festive lights losing their magic if they stay up after the party is over.

When anticipation is high and imagination vivid, a promising parcel can produce great expectations, and disappointment can follow hard on the heels of hopes that are too high. So we learn early on that gifts are not necessarily all they seem: the simplest gift can be the most exciting, and the plainest parcel may contain the most surprising and wonderful reward. In time, and with guidance, children learn not to expect, but to be open to receiving and always to appreciate, in which case they may be pleasantly surprised and rarely disappointed.

Simple Ways to Create a Personal Gift

- Take a special photograph, and get family, friends, or colleagues to sign the mount. It will immediately become precious, even before you put it in a frame. (This idea came from my cousin Nicole, who corralled our entire family for this purpose before a very special wedding.)

- Buy real ribbon made of natural fiber to tie up your parcels. It often costs no more than synthetic ribbon, and it makes your gift look extra-special. If possible, deliver the packages in person.

- Bake! Homemade cookies or cake are always welcome, even if you are not a confident baker.

- Create a simple posy of handpicked flowers, grasses, or leaves, containing an odd number of each element, such as three or five.

- Give something away. Most of us own far more than we need. As adults we may be hanging on to items that were precious to us in younger years—clothes or toys or paraphernalia from long-lost hobbies—but that someone else could be gaining pleasure from now.

gratitude guru: **Martin Seligman**

The internationally renowned psychologist Professor Martin Seligman is director of the Penn Positive Psychology Center at Pennsylvania State University. Professor Seligman has devised a series of measures that help to prove that those with a "can do" attitude, who believe that they have control over their life, and who understand that they can choose how to respond to adversity or obstacles, tend to be in better physical health and more resilient. Optimistic people are not necessarily more grateful than pessimists. However, research is showing that practicing gratitude may be the key to enabling pessimists to become more optimistic.

"I don't think you can have a positive future unless you can envision one."

Martin Seligman (1942–)

Receiving

When someone gives a gift or gives of themselves,
someone else receives and accepts what that person
wished to share. Giving and receiving are the yin and
yang of the exchange. Neither can exist without the
other. It is a balanced ritual that extends back beyond
the dawn of the world's religions.

> *"We cannot hold a torch
> to light another person's
> path without shining
> light to guide our own
> way too."*
>
> Anonymous

The Perpetual Gratitude Jar

Create a personal pot of gratitude with ideas for ways to say thank you. This can be a real jar or a metaphorical jar, depending on whether you want a physical reminder or whether the act of contemplating the jar is enough to focus your thoughts.

1. Random gratitude method

Add names of those you wish to thank on pieces of paper of one color, and ways to say thank you on pieces of paper of another color. Choose two pieces of paper, one of each color, to marry up ideas for giving.

2. Focused gratitude method

The pot is the ideal place to turn all your guilty "shoulds" into positive action—write down specific ideas and choose one at random every so often. For example:

Take Lily to the mall this weekend.

Treat Mom to a girls' lunch.

Bake Tom a birthday cake this year.

Phone Maud to find out about her health.

Book a weekend to see Grandma.

Put together a surprise care package for Mike.

Gratitude in Practice

Seeing the positive

Marion recalls a time when she was given a spinning wheel as a gift from an elderly friend who could no longer spin. "I was so delighted with the gift," she says, "that I over-did the spinning and developed an injury that prevented me from pursuing my other love: music. It took time, but I was eventually able to feel gratitude for the downtime as it allowed me to read more and to pay attention by listening to music, and also to start learning a new language—none of which I had time for previously."

*"It is not happiness
that makes us
grateful; it is
gratefulness that
makes us happy."*

David Steindl-Rast (1926–)

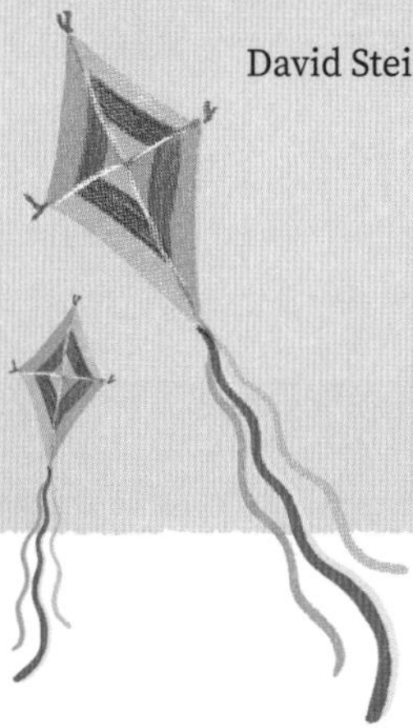

"In the best, the friendliest and simplest relations, flattery or praise is necessary, just as grease is necessary to keep wheels turning."

Leo Tolstoy (1828–1910), *War and Peace*

The Joy of Thanks

The foundations of gratitude begin in childhood. Young children's thank-you letters are often a joy—free-flowing and half-formed, short on spelling, with a few crayon scribbles for illustrative effect, they are often tucked away lovingly and kept for years by the recipient. When children say thank you, they pause to appreciate what has been given to them and remember in a more conscious way the fact that they have been valued.

Of course, few children actually enjoy writing thank-you letters, and that makes it hard for parents when they try to insist that they should. But for the giver who has put heart and time into choosing and wrapping the gift, a silence shouts not only a lack of thankfulness, but also a lack of care. The strength of feeling that the giver poured into giving the gift is reabsorbed as a negative reward. Even those who swear that they were not expecting a thank you will be affected in this way. Saying thank you is good for us. It helps to "seal the deal," as those early traders understood.

Did You Know?

The University of California, Berkeley, runs the grateful-sounding Greater Good Science Center, which funds research into the long-term benefits of gratitude. Scientists at the center have discovered that people who practice gratitude regularly have been found to:

- Develop stronger immune systems and lower blood pressure

- Experience higher levels of positive emotion

- Have an increased sense of joy, optimism, and happiness

- Be more likely to act with generosity and compassion

- Feel less lonely and isolated

Visit their website to find out more about the latest research in this area (see Resources, page 140).

Ebb and Flow

Sometimes a gift is so generous that accepting it can be difficult—
house repairs, a loan for a car, college fees, babysitting, lifts to
hospital. Barriers get in the way of acceptance, such as fear of
feeling beholden, a sense of unworthiness, worries about not being
able to reciprocate, or loss of self-respect. However, my father has
a lovely philosophy about giving and receiving, which he refers to
as "ebb and flow." All it means is that energy, time, money, and
companionship are all resources that are needed at different ages
and stages of life, and all can be exchanged as time goes by.

The Gratitude Tree

Trees of all shapes and species are a wonderful symbol of the way that gratitude grows and envelops and nourishes us, providing the oxygen we need to thrive and survive.

The gratitude tree is sown from seeds of kindness and spreads via the roots of belonging. Gratitude grows like the solid trunk of an ancient oak, generating connectedness through its branches via the acts of giving, receiving, and reciprocating. As it matures over the seasons, the beautiful foliage of acceptance emerges, creating a canopy of ever-varying color and offering protection to all, and of course it bears the fruit of love, friendship, happiness, and forgiveness—that germinate further acts of kindness and spread the roots of gratitude further.

For the gratitude tree to thrive, there is an additional nutrient required in the earth that feeds the roots—and that is trust. Trust that the gifts are bestowed with no artificial additive of expectation; and that the tree will be nurtured with goodwill and watered with appreciation to protect it from neglect or drought.

Giving Thanks for Skills and Abilities

A sense of gratitude can be developed consciously, either as a coping strategy when life does not turn out quite as planned, or simply as a way of appreciating the "here and now."

List three skills and abilities that you feel grateful for. You may like to include:

1. A note of why you appreciate these talents.

2. An observation or compliment made by someone else that you can accept wholeheartedly.

3. A deeper thought about your vision for your skills and talents in the future.

1. _____

2. _____

3. _____

Unsung Heroes

Who are the people whose work you benefit from each day, who are rarely acknowledged for their dedication? For example:

- The cleaner who focuses on the craftsmanship that went into making the sweep of the staircase that she dusts every day, instead of seeing her repetitive work as a chore.

- The nurse who has a waiting room full of patients, but still manages to greet every single person by name and with a smile, instead of focusing on the number of blood samples he has taken that day.

- The receptionist at the motel who speaks directly to your elderly mother and connects with her sense of humor, rather than judging her for her age and her wheelchair.

"Life isn't all ha ha hee hee."

Meera Syal CBE (1961–), writer and actor

CHAPTER 4

acceptance
(or when gratitude is difficult)

Sometimes in life we are pitched a curveball. It can be hard to feel any sense of gratitude in the midst of a tragedy, illness, or disaster. But it is when we have the most to lose that we also have the most to gain. When life as we know it is torn away, we are left with a greater awareness of what is most important. This section takes a good look at how to cope when gratitude is difficult, and offers ways to reframe life's challenges with hope and forgiveness—and generosity.

When Times are Hard

In the words of the gratitude expert Robert Emmons, "Life is suffering. No amount of positive thinking exercises will change this truth." He acknowledges clearly through his research that forcibly adopting an artificially positive stance during times of trauma can have the opposite effect. "Keep calm and carry on" might be the only mantra you can manage at times of pressure.

Gratitude in Practice

Keeping faith

On August 5, 2010, in Atacama, Chile, 33 miners were trapped underground when part of a mine collapsed, leaving all exit routes blocked. Dismay turned to hope when the rescue team found a note that told anxious families that the miners were alive. Sixty-nine days later, following a remarkable feat of skilled engineering, all the miners were rescued to a sense of overwhelming gratitude that was felt the world over.

Thought Swapping

- If you find yourself thinking, *"I am so fed up that X happened,"* try swapping it with, *"At least I can be glad that Y didn't happen."*

- *"I am so fed up with having to chase my kids to get out of bed every morning,"* could become, *"I am so glad that my kids are still young enough to need me—but it is time they learned to take personal responsibility for getting themselves up in the morning."*

- *"I wish people didn't come to me to offload all their problems,"* might become, *"I hope I helped in some way, and it is good to know that I am trusted."*

- Feeling that *"I am so tired of having to go to the doctor for tests"* is completely understandable, but it becomes easier to handle if it is reframed as, *"I am glad to have these tests underway and am grateful that the doctor is taking them seriously."*

> ## *"Opportunity is the gift within every gift."*
>
> David Steindl-Rast (1926–)

Letting Go

Anyone who has faced a painful loss of any kind will know the mixed emotions that can arise, and how hard it can be to step forward into a new phase of life. Sometimes we get stuck in a cycle of looking backward, with regret, guilt, anger, or sadness. In the words of the British novelist L.P. Hartley, "The past is a foreign country: they do things differently there." Focusing on might-have-beens has the potential to cut us off from future possibilities. In the short term, the gracious way to reframe your thought processes is by seeking positivity amid the difficulty.

- *"I am grateful to have discovered that I am stronger and more resilient than I realized."*

- *"I'm so glad for what we had. We had a lot of fun together and I am grateful for those happy times."*

- *"I appreciate the way my partner put the children's needs before his own when we divorced."*

- *"I will be eternally grateful for the gracious kindness and attention that we received from the hospital's care team."*

Gratitude in Practice

Experiencing freedom

Robin, 44, is a recovering cancer patient. "Extreme suffering becomes in the end a form of liberation. When you have nothing left to lose you no longer care what anyone thinks. When you no longer fear death, you are free to live the better life that you always wanted." He and his family have found a new sense of gratitude in the simple joy of being in each other's company. "The little things no longer irritate;" says Robin's wife. "Every day feels more precious now."

Crossing the Bridge

Many of us have been brought up to be stoical in the face of problems or adversity. Brits, especially, are known for their "stiff upper lip" under pressure (that is, not showing emotion). Independence builds walls, not bridges. If you find yourself habitually consumed by disappointment, with few expectations of hope or happiness, don't suffer in silence. Talk to friends to get a new perspective, or have a chat with your doctor. There may be other ways to help you get through this temporary tough time. Working together or discussing problems provides a broader perspective. Collaboration and conversation are the bridges that generate new perspective and understanding that is greater than anything we could imagine alone, and in doing so we put competition and ego aside. We feel grateful for the outcome. Gratitude is a leveler. It reminds us that we are all connected and part of something greater than ourselves.

A Franciscan Blessing

(Thirteenth century)

May you be blessed with discomfort at easy answers, half-truths, and superficial relationships—so that you may live deep within your heart.

May you be blessed with anger at injustice, oppression, and exploitation of people—so that you may work for justice, freedom, and peace.

May you be blessed with tears shed for those who suffer pain, rejection, hunger, and war—so that you may reach out your hand to comfort them and turn their pain to joy.

May you be blessed with enough foolishness to believe that you can make a difference to the world—so that you can do what others claim cannot be done, to bring justice and kindness to our children and to the poor.

Combating Cynicism

In her book *The Business Alchemist*, Pilar Godino talks about each of us being motivated either to move toward or away from something in our conversation. Toward sentences are full of positivity and connection; away from sentences are negative and pull away from the risk of being hurt. For example:

- *"My son only ever calls me when he wants something"* is an away from sentence. The corresponding toward statement is *"I have a good relationship with my son and I love it when he calls. He knows that I will say no if I cannot help."*

- *"My sister only gave me the furniture because she no longer has space for it"* (away from), instead of, *"She is a star for giving me first refusal"* (toward).

- *"If I hadn't called my friend she would not have invited me"* (away from), instead of, *"The party should be fun. I need to keep in touch better"* (toward).

Becoming aware of how we use language when we talk to ourselves can be a surprisingly strong way to bring more gratitude into our lives and relationships.

I Wish, I Want …

You may like to take a moment to think of something
you want or that you wish you had. Do these desires
feel like a goal that you can achieve, or an entitlement
that you lack? Notice how this makes you feel,
and even how your posture responds or your facial
expression changes as you contemplate your wishes.

Positive Thinking

Being "glad" may not be a panacea for future happiness, and "thinking positive" doesn't guarantee that everything will turn out all right, but it does seems that conscious gratitude is connected to optimism and forgiveness, which are likely to lead to positive action and eventual change.

Taking Stock
Try taking a moment to complete the following sentences:

I am grateful that _____

happened because _____

_____

I am grateful to _____

because _____

I am grateful for this moment because _____

_____

Gratitude is not necessarily an immediate response. Sometimes the statements need to be repeated, to enable you to drill deeper, and to still the quiet voice of resistance. Over time, and with practice, when feelings of anger or impatience surface, having a few gratitude anchors in your mental armory can help to diffuse an uncomfortable or upsetting situation.

Choosing Change

Think about how you can actively work toward change
by trying to complete the lists below.

Three things I feel dissatisfied with that I can change positively:

1. _____

2. _____

_____

Two people who could help me to look at my
situation in another way:

1. _____

2. _____

One thing I can start to change from today:

1. _____

_____

"*As we express our gratitude, we must never forget that the highest appreciation is not to utter words, but to live by them.*"

John F. Kennedy (1917–1963), politician and

35th President of the United States

CHAPTER 5

Showing appreciation

True gratitude has a way of generating a warm sense of appreciation. But what does this really mean? The literal meaning of appreciation is to price something. When we say thank you in appreciation, we are saying clearly, "I put a great value on what you have done," and when we are moved to take action because we appreciate what someone is going through, we are expressing an understanding of the true cost of their experiences—in every sense of the word.

An action that is offered in gratitude and received with appreciation seals the deal. It becomes an equal exchange.

Taking Action

Gratitude is a habit that we must cultivate constantly if we are to gain the benefits. Developing the gratitude habit starts by paying attention to the people who are in our life every day, and offering them expressions of appreciation and kindness. It moves on to appreciating ourselves and the role we play in our own relationships, as well as the world at large and all the creatures and beauty within it. It begins, however, with small steps, and with focusing on the everyday.

"Have I told you lately (that I love you)?"

Van Morrison, 1989

Making Time for Family

Relationships within families can be complicated, and may change over time. Even when we are fortunate enough to have strong bonds with our siblings, cousins, or parents, the chances are that we take our loved ones for granted much of the time. One of the easiest ways of showing gratitude, especially to parents and grandparents, is simply to offer them the gift of your time. That means time with full attention intact, and possibly a strong dose of patience, too—with both ears in action (especially if you are talking by phone).

- Do you have a relative whom you have not seen for some time? Is it time to give him or her a call to show your appreciation?

- How much of your life do you share with your parents and grandparents? Do you involve them to some extent, or are you living in a parallel universe?

- How much do you know about their lives? For example, do you know what they studied at school or whether they enjoyed sport?

- How often do you ask them to tell you about their past? How did they meet? What is their story?

- When you think back over your life, what have you learned from your parents, and what childhood moments do you feel grateful for?

- If there were troubled times, are you able to find ways to understand with appreciation and forgiveness in your heart? We are on this little planet for too short a spell not to make the most of the time we have together, even if the going gets tough and we fall out sometimes.

Gratitude in Practice

Kindness and inspiration

Gratitude stems from kindness and inspiration that appear in unexpected places. At a time when the deadline for this book was getting ever nearer, I was due to stay with some great friends. I was looking forward to seeing them but extremely anxious about the impact on my work. It had been a challenging time—my ancient computer had decided to give up the ghost and I was behind schedule. Then my car broke down. There was no way I could go. However, being the kind of people they are, they wouldn't take no for an answer, and insisted on driving 50 miles out of their way to come and pick me up.

En route to me, their vehicle broke down as well. Oh no! I received a disappointed text: "Sorry—but this one really is out of our hands." (I was secretly rather relieved!) Rather wonderfully, however, their insurance covered the provision of a hire car. They came to get me anyway. After a lovely meal and great conversation, I pleaded work and headed for the guest room, at the top of the house. The walls were painted a deep blue, and covered in fluorescent stars that would begin glowing mysteriously when the lights went out. It had once been their daughter's room and was very peaceful. On the wall was a notice, which read: "Every day may not be good, but there is something good in every day." This is the perfect place for me to be, I thought—and sat down to write.

The Joy of Friends

Do you ever take the people you care about for granted?

• When you think of your friendship circle, do some people get the fun assignments while others get the angst?

• When you get in touch, do you respect their time? Or do you expect them to "drop everything" and be there for you?

The person whom you turn toward to talk through your woes is not always the same person you choose to go partying with, although you probably appreciate them equally. Showing conscious appreciation is an important part of building friendships and becomes increasingly important as we get older.

The Power of Laughter

Gratitude often has a light, upbeat energy. Anyone who has ever seen a video of wise elders such as Nelson Mandela or Archbishop Desmond Tutu will know that even when they were talking about serious matters, they were never far from humor and sharing the sound of laughter. Sara Algoe has undertaken research in this area, too, and has found that laughter plays a crucial role in the way human beings relate to and appreciate one another. We feel closer to those who share our sense of humor. When we can share a belly laugh, we get on much better and work together more cooperatively. Could this finding provide a revolutionary approach to improving international relations and achieving world peace?

"Find.

Remind.

Bind."

Professor Sara Algoe PhD, University of North Carolina

Appreciating One Another

It is easy to show appreciation:

- "I really appreciated your beautiful/kind/unexpected/
generous/delightful gift. I can just imagine the trouble
you went to in finding it."

- "I really appreciated your kind support during such a
difficult time—especially as you have your own challenges
at the moment."

- "I truly appreciate you coming with me today. I know
how busy you are at the moment."

- "We so appreciate you sharing our day. I know many
of you have traveled a very long way to be here."

- "I love and appreciate you for all that you have done
for me during the course of my life. I know you have
put aside many of your own plans for our benefit."

Gratitude in Practice

In the workplace

Alex is a consultant who helps businesses to turn their finances around. He says, "There are no villains—or very rarely. When things go wrong it is usually because people have been trying to do their best, not their worst. However, over time what was previously the best way may no longer be the most effective way. Ultimately people tend to be full of gratitude for the opportunity to speak up about their problems, because they care a great deal and want things to turn out well."

A Call to Action

We tend to show appreciation for the things we attach most importance to. When we become focused primarily on ourselves and our own needs, the world loses balance. However, practicing gratitude consciously encourages us to connect with and feel grateful for the world around us. When we feel connected, we begin to notice more clearly what is going on—and to see when things are out of balance. Gratitude can therefore lead us to take action, to try to improve life not only for ourselves but also for others, because we begin to see very clearly that we are all part of the same universe. No man is an island.

"Your energy will flow to where your attention goes."

Anonymous

Horatio's Garden

In Salisbury, England, there is a beautiful garden full of structural plants and striking sculptures. However, there are several unusual things about this garden:

• Its location. It is on a prime plot at the main district hospital: an oasis of calm that flourishes not far from the spinal treatment center, and within strolling distance of the visitor parking lots near by.

• Its conception: it was the brainchild of a very gifted and energetic young man called Horatio. A prospective medical student, he was only 17 when he spent a summer volunteering at the hospital, helping to feed and care for patients recovering from spinal injuries. He saw immediately that they needed somewhere to escape to, where they could relax and be themselves during their long recovery. After doing his research and gaining evidence of patients' needs and wishes, he used his initiative to lobby the chief executive with his idea.

• Sadly, there is a third reason that the garden is unusual. In a tragic accident, Horatio was attacked and killed by a polar bear while on a schools' expedition in Norway the following summer. That's not something any parent expects or can ever fully come to terms with.

The garden, by the award-winning designer Cleve West, is testament to an outpouring of gratitude for Horatio's energetic and vibrant young life, and appreciation for his inspired idea. Horatio's family were overwhelmed by the extraordinary wave of kindness and support received in the form of donations from those who had read the story of Horatio's death. Soon, his parents hope, there will be eleven Horatio's gardens at spinal units around Britain.

Although Horatio's story is on the website of his charity (see Resources, page 140), Horatio's Garden, and woven into the fabric of the garden in Salisbury, it is humbling to see that the family's tragedy is not center stage. The focus of the organization is kept quite deliberately on the present-day patients and their recovery. Horatio's garden as a concept has taken off, and Horatio's legacy is one of recovery and remembrance—one that will be appreciated for generations.

"You have not lived today
until you have done
something for someone
who can never repay you."

John Bunyan (1628–1688)

Whistle While You Work

Does your work area reflect the time and effort that you put in to each working day? Many people have photographs of loved ones on their desktop to help to remind them of their greater motivation, but what about including symbols of gratitude for all that you do?

• Expand the gratitude culture. Do you take time to acknowledge a colleague who has something to celebrate? Do you take a moment to say thank you or to show your appreciation, even for the small things? Do you show appreciation publicly for great work and support? Never assume that no one will care or notice.

• If someone shows you appreciation, do you savor the experience with gratitude and keep those flowers, that gift, the card, in plain sight—or do you tuck things away modestly in a drawer? Symbols of gratitude can help others to raise their game, too, and the whole team to feel valued.

• Do you feel grateful for your working environment? How much creative mess is good for your head? Some people's idea of order is a meticulously tidy workspace; others appreciate a bit of color and creativity. Does your work area feed stress or soothe it? How could you change it for the better?

• Make an effort to remember people's names—especially the names of those who are new to the organization. We all suffer from temporary amnesia from time to time but knowing the names of those you work alongside is an important sign that you value their presence and contribution.

The Gift of Praise

Take a moment to appreciate your family, friends, neighbors, and colleagues—honoring those who contribute to your world in the broadest sense:

- Who in your life deserves praise for something achieved or well done?

- What have you done that you can quietly praise yourself for?

- Is there someone in your community who deserves positive praise and feedback for all the hard work they put in, without much recognition?

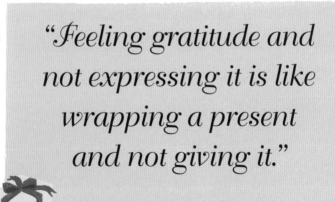

"Feeling gratitude and not expressing it is like wrapping a present and not giving it."

William Arthur Ward (1921–1994), writer

Take a Journal Moment

The following questions may take time and consideration to answer.

- Who do you turn to during a time of turmoil?

- Who knows you better than you know yourself and loves you for who you are?

- Who tends to be there for you, no matter what?

- Who is your lifeline for the big stuff?

- Who keeps you sane with the little stuff?

- Who has made a difference to your life?

- Who has listened to your cares and worries without expecting anything in return?

- Who do you appreciate who does not always get shown appreciation?

- Who may be needing your support right now?

- Whom do you appreciate for the care they offer to others?

- Who would value you paying them greater attention, and cares when you are not around?

- How can you show someone close to you how much you care about and appreciate them?

"Gratitude is not only the greatest of virtues, but the parent of all the others."

Marcus Tullius Cicero (106–43 BCE),

philosopher and theorist

CHAPTER 6

sharing and thanksgiving

Every culture has traditions and festivals that involve sharing and celebration. From Thanksgiving to Christmas, Hanukkah to Diwali, Easter to Eid-al-Fitr, the Chinese Moon Festival to the Ghanaian Homowo Yam Festival, we have always given thanks for the harvest, for the seasons, for day and night, for our health and well-being, for spiritual nourishment, and for the food on our table.

Festivals Across the World

Giving thanks is embedded in the ceremonies of every spiritual tradition in the world. In early times, this may have involved more superstitious forms of worship, with forms of sacrifice and ritual that we would not embrace today, but nevertheless, recognizing that we are not alone is an important aspect of being human.

In America

An "attitude of gratitude" helps everyone to face the world in a positive and upbeat way, so it is no surprise that feelings of goodwill expand even farther when everyone gathers to celebrate and appreciate at the same time. Taking the time to be consciously aware of all that matters and to give thanks to those we love and care for—and even to those we find more challenging—is a great way to build bridges, reach joint understanding, and bring families and communities together. Thanksgiving helps us to move beyond petty differences and remember the wonder of life and what really matters to us all.

As every American will know, the Thanksgiving feast dates back to November 1621, when the newly arrived Pilgrims shared simple food with the local Wampanoag tribe. In Canada, Thanksgiving started even earlier, in 1578. It is credited to the English explorer Martin Frobisher, who with his men gave thanks for their safe return to harbor after their expedition through the country's icy northern wastes to find the great Northwest Passage. Since those early days, the annual tradition of sharing turkey, pumpkin pie, and other holiday treats has reunited families and friends across the whole continent.

Pumpkin Pie is Made for Sharing

Ingredients

1 medium pumpkin, halved and seeds removed

2 eggs, plus an extra egg yolk

½ cup/170g soft brown sugar

1 heaped cup/115g superfine (caster) sugar

½ tsp salt

2 tsp cinnamon

1 tsp ground ginger

¼ tsp each ground nutmeg and ground cloves

¼ tsp ground cardamom (optional)

grated zest of half a lemon

1½ cups/350ml heavy (double) cream (or a 12-oz/350-ml can unsweetened condensed milk)

1 sweet shortcrust ready-made pastry shell, 9in./23cm in diameter

Serves 8

Method

1. Preheat the oven to 350°F/180°C/Gas 4.

2. First make the pumpkin purée: line a baking sheet with greaseproof paper or baking parchment. Place the pumpkin halves cut side down on the sheet and bake for 1–1½ hours, until the flesh is soft and can be easily pierced. Remove from the oven and allow to cool before scooping out the pulp. (For extra-smooth purée, push through a strainer/sieve before use.) Turn the oven up to 425°F/220°C/Gas 7.

3. Beat the eggs and egg yolk in a large bowl. Mix in the sugars, salt, spices, and lemon zest.

4. Add the pumpkin purée (making sure it is completely cool). Stir in the cream, and beat everything together until well mixed.

5. Pour the filling into the pastry shell, making sure it is spread nice and thickly (to allow for shrinkage as it cooks).

6. Bake for 15 minutes, then lower the temperature to 350°F/180°C/ Gas 4 and bake for 45–55 minutes more.

7. To check whether the pie is ready, insert a skewer into the center of the filling. If it comes out clean, the pie is cooked. If not, bake for a few more minutes before testing again.

8. Leave the pie to cool and relax on a wire rack, then cut into slices. For extra decadence, serve with whipped cream, ice cream, or yogurt.

Spiritual Traditions

Giving thanks is embedded in the religious ceremonies of every spiritual tradition in the world.

Diwali (mid-October to mid-November, depending on the lunar year)

This festival of lights is a beautiful occasion and very important in the Hindu, Sikh, and Jain calendars. A festival of prayers and a day for exchanging sweets and goodwill, it is an official holiday in many countries. In the Hindu faith, Diwali uses light to symbolize the overcoming of ignorance that brings darkness to the world, and celebrates stepping toward the light of knowledge, understanding, and self-awareness.

Hanukkah (late December to early January)

This eight-day Jewish festival also marks the beginning of a new year, and it too uses light to symbolize thanksgiving and gratitude. Each of the eight candles in the Menorah is lit in a precise way and in a particular order each night of the festival, and burns for half an hour after nightfall.

Eid-al-Fitr (Festival of the Breaking of the Fast)

This festival in the Muslim calendar marks the end of Ramadan, an important time of prayer and fasting. Eid is celebrated on the first day of the month of Shawwal. It is a day of prayer and forgiveness—and the only day when fasting is forbidden. On this day it is expected that as much charity as possible will be given, happily, to the poor and others in need.

Christmas (December 25)

Traditionally, Christmas Day also represented the breaking of a fast. In the Eastern Orthodox Church, fasting would continue throughout Advent, culminating in a strict fast on the eve of the Nativity (Christmas Eve). In the modern, secular world, many have moved away from this tradition, but the focus of thanksgiving still lies in the sharing of a meal with family, friends, and strangers.

Birthday Gifts that Give

- The next time you have a birthday to celebrate, consider giving gifts to others instead of waiting to receive them!

- Instead of giving gifts to each other, consider giving time or money to a humanitarian cause or a welfare organization.

- Pass on a gift that has had meaning for you in the past: perhaps you were given a piece of jewelry, a book, a pen, or an ornament for a significant birthday, which you love but no longer use. Do you know someone who is the same age as you were then who would enjoy it?

Gratitude in Practice

Celebrating good times and great memories

We are so fortunate to be living in an age where it is possible to share photos, stories, and memories so widely and so quickly.

"I create a photographic calendar each year as a Christmas present for the family, which records key moments of the year (and includes everyone's birthdays, too!). The grandparents really appreciate it and always look forward to it." Sue

"For my daughter's 21st birthday I created a photo record of her life with captions and stories. She loved it and was so grateful as it reminded her of her early days." Nicole

"My father was a very talented artist, though very modest about his skills. I decided to have a number of his pictures turned into cards. We have had so much positive feedback that I am going to create some more." Phil

Host a Celebration—
Large or Small

Although holidays and birthdays provide set times to celebrate and
be grateful, remember that you can celebrate at any time of year.
Whatever kind of shared celebration you are planning, it does not
have to be stressful. Remember that gratitude is all about sharing
the load, so here are a few things to keep in mind:

1. Instead of planning for "perfect," aim to expect—and accept—
the unexpected!

2. Accept with gratitude as much help on the day as your kitchen
can accommodate.

3. Put yourself first at a key point in the day, so that you have
showered and dressed and are feeling relaxed with plenty
of time to spare.

Party Preparation

On the more practical side of things, here are a few tips
to get you started:

- Be prepared! Planning prevents last-minute stresses
and headaches.

- It is a good idea to set the table the evening before
(and, if you have a pet or a small child with curious fingers,
keep everything lightly covered and protected).

- When it comes to the food, stick to your favorite recipes.

- Do as much as possible ahead of time, by planning the menu
well in advance and preparing as much food beforehand as
you can.

- Don't try to provide everything yourself, though.
A gathering where everyone has contributed is
always remembered warmly, and it shares the strain
of preparation and the pressure of the expense.

- Refreshments should be planned in
advance, too—once everyone has a drink in
their hand, they won't mind waiting for the meal.

- Chilling the glasses in the fridge or freezer gives
them a dramatic frosted appearance and helps to keep the
drinks cool.

- Too much formality can prevent people from relaxing.

I am Thinking of You

Have you ever received a gift or a gesture out of the blue? Do you remember how it made you feel? Unexpected gifts as gestures of kindness and support can be the most memorable, uplifting, and heartwarming of all.

A simple posy of flowers, a care parcel in the form of tea and cake, an invitation to lunch, a text, or a phone call: there are numerous ways to reach out spontaneously to show our friends how much we care about them. Receiving a card unexpectedly from someone you haven't heard from for a long time can really make your day.

- Do you know someone who is going through a difficult time, who could do with an act of kindness or some moral support?

- Do you want to let someone know you are thinking about them?

- Is there someone in your life who has been generous or supportive without expecting anything in return?

- Who needs you to share some goodwill with them today?

"Hope smiles from the threshold of the year to come, whispering 'it will be happier'..."

Alfred, Lord Tennyson (1809–1892)

Blessing of Gratitude

This blessing is by Buddhist practitioner Jack Kornfield.

Let yourself sit quietly and in a relaxed fashion. Take a deep breath and then let go. Let your heart feel easy.

Allow your body to let go of all tension and become ready to receive this blessing:

I offer my gratitude to the universe and all that is in it, for

the friends I have been given;

the family I have been given;

my life and all that I have been given.

Now continue to breathe in and out gently. Picture someone you care about, and think about them as they go about their daily life—and about the happiness and success you wish for them. With each breath, offer them your thanks from the bottom of your heart:

May you always have joy in your heart.

May you always enjoy good fortune.

May your happiness continue to increase.

May you always have peace and well-being on this earth.

"*Wear gratitude like a cloak and it will sustain every corner of your life.*"

Rumi (1207–1273), poet and mystic

CHAPTER 7

Seeking Contentment

Living a life of gratitude is both incredibly simple and, on occasion, extremely challenging—and sometimes both at the same time. The challenges occur because we have a tendency to hold on tightly to negative emotions, such as resentment, anger, and fear that prevent us from feeling wholehearted gratitude and contentment. The simplicity lies in the realization that once we let go of those feelings and recognize the power and beauty of acceptance, it is possible for the barriers to gratitude to fade away.

The Danger of Entitlement

Much of the discontent and unhappiness we feel in life is connected to the things we do not have. When we compare our own situation with other people's we will always be left wanting—not least because we don't know the full picture. We don't really know what anyone else's life is actually like. However, the magic is that disappointment and dissatisfaction are not always negative; they can also become a driving force that leads us to strive and to achieve. By taking stock when we feel negative, we can choose to focus on gratitude in the form of feeling thankful for future possibilities instead.

When we expect less and appreciate more, something interesting happens: levels of satisfaction about small things become higher. The child who has strived to improve on a D grade is thrilled with their C and starts to see a B as possible; the person who earns very little appreciates every penny of a performance bonus and has faith in their prospects for the future. Letting go of the idea that we are entitled and swapping it for a feeling of appreciation is a powerful step toward inner contentment and happiness.

Gratitude in Practice
Giving away the past

"I love my books and had built up a substantial collection—many from college and school days," says Tammy. "The idea of giving any of them away was anathema to me. They were part of who I am—or so I thought. When I came to move home in my fifties I started to browse through some of the books as I packed them. I realized that not only was the typeface far too small for my aging eyes, it was also the first time I had leafed through the pages in 30 years! I decided to take radical action before I had a chance to change my mind. I photographed the books' spines so I could re-order favorite titles online, and took several boxes of books to goodwill stores. The charity volunteers were grateful to have such a useful windfall, my husband was grateful that our removal storage charges would not be quite as high, and as an added bonus our grandchildren were very proud that I had finally discovered the joy of reading books online and had made it into the twenty-first century. A positive result all round."

Making Amends

Most families and friends experience misunderstandings from time to time, but sometimes these transform into full-blown estrangement. Years may pass without contact, until no one really understands why the disagreement happened any more. Each "side" waits for the other to take the first step toward forgiveness, and meanwhile each has a lesser life without the other in it.

As human beings we are remarkable. We have free will and the power of conscious choice. We can choose our responses. Every one of us has the power to create change within ourselves, and to reach out to others to put things right. Making amends requires someone to make a positive choice—to risk a moment of rejection by putting another person's needs before their own. The chances are that once you have reached out, even if there is a period of unsettled adjustment, there will be a reciprocal sense of gratitude that you have been in contact and that a bridge has been built.

"*Count your blessings (instead of sheep).*"

Irving Berlin, 1954

Gratitude Through Fulfillment

Those who know what it is to become a parent for the first time understand the overwhelming sense of wonder, love, and gratitude that having a baby son or daughter can generate—and how that bond produces a sense of love and fulfillment through the ups and downs of life. For others, the experience of creating, developing, or contributing through work may lead to a powerful sense of accomplishment and happiness. Gratitude for our own contentment generates kindness toward others. When we feel a sense of belonging, we want to keep everyone safe and make sure their needs are met.

Gratitude in Practice

Looking fear in the face

On the afternoon of October 9, 2012, Malala
Yousafzai was taking her usual bus home from school
in Pakistan when she was shot in the head. She had
been targeted as punishment for writing about life
under the Taliban in a public blog, which had been
publicized by the BBC in Britain. She recovered from
her injuries, and has since then been given several
prestigious awards, including the Nobel Peace Prize.
She is now appreciated and respected everywhere
as an ambassador for peace. There are hundreds
of women around the world who are grateful for her
courage and her example.

Your Life as Legacy

- What can you be grateful for that you would like others to share in and to benefit from?

- What are the "lessons in life" that you would like to share so that others have the chance to see life through your eyes?

- Where have you traveled and what have you seen that might fascinate and interest future generations?

- What mistakes have you made that you are grateful for because you have learned from them, and that others might learn from too?

- Which people in your life have had a positive impact on you, whose memory you would like to keep alive?

- Who would you like to share these memories with so that they can benefit the next generation, too?

gratitude guru: **David Steindl-Rast**

No book on gratitude is complete without mentioning David Steindl-Rast OSB, an Austrian-born Catholic Benedictine monk with a peaceful and mesmeric voice, who cofounded a center for spiritual studies in 1968 with teachers from the Buddhist, Sufi, Hindu, and Jewish faiths. Brother David also cofounded the nonprofit A Network for Grateful Living, which is dedicated to gratefulness as a route to transformation in all societies. His videos and talks are an inspirational joy for everyone who is on a mission to live life more thankfully (see Resources, page 140).

> *"Stop. Look. Go.*
> *That's all."*

David Steindl-Rast (1926–)

Success and Gratitude

It is very important to stop and take a moment to acknowledge life's milestones. How can we stride forward with clarity unless we know where we are in relation to where we began—and give thanks for getting to this point? The following symbols of success and gratitude also represent important rites of passage:

Medals and trophies—Usually hard-won, they represent a moment when striving for personal goals and competing against the best delivers wonderful results, and they are received with gratitude.

Birthdays—Not always welcomed as we get older, they are nevertheless important. They are symbolic celebrations that represent rites of passage—each year of our life and the love, appreciation, and gratitude that others have for our presence on this earth.

Examination results—of every sort. They represent the gratitude that you might choose to show to your teachers for taking you to this point, to your parents for supporting you, and to yourself for your achievements.

♥ ♥ ♥ ♥ ♥ ♥ ♥

Gratitude Happy-Tude

Sometimes we spend so much time measuring personal happiness against other people's achievements or expectations that we overlook the joys we already have. There is a profound connection between gratitude and contentment.

List three things that make you want to shout out in happiness (or at the very least always make you smile):

1. _____

2. _____

3. _____

My Gratitude Challenge

This one needs time to think about and plan. Many people who have taken up a large-scale challenge have done so because they want to give back in some way or to offer support. We all know people who have taken action to walk, run, swim, climb, or skydive, or who have undertaken some other tremendous feat for the benefit of a cause. Choosing a challenge for the good of others has the benefit of helping other people to get the "feel-good factor" by helping you, sponsoring you, and sharing in the glory of your success. The impact can be personally transformative, too.

"I climbed Mount Kilimanjaro to celebrate my 60th birthday and to test my resilience, while also raising money for my local hospital. On the trip I also happened to meet the man who would become my husband, which was a joy-filled bonus!" Vanda

"I wanted to challenge myself by running a half-marathon and it was the perfect way to raise funds for the hospice that cared for our family friend, Aunty Margaret, too. The training was tough, but I loved taking part in the event and am ready to train for my next event now!" Libby

Is there something you could undertake for a good cause? Try sitting with the idea for a little while. You will know when it is right for you to take action.

Your Gratitude Portrait

Liz Handy is a talented photographer who has developed an interesting way of creating self-portraits. She invites her subjects to select six objects that define different areas of their life, plus a flower.

Your gratitude portrait has a similar mission, with a slight twist: the objects you choose must be things that represent the areas of your life, or the people, that you value and are grateful for.

To start your own gratitude portrait, ask yourself, or write in your journal:

- Which three people in my life have I learned the most from, and why?

- Which two people (outside my immediate family) need me the most today?

- Which author/artist/poet/musician/engineer/scientist have I always admired without taking the time to explore or enjoy his/her work? Start today!

Focusing on Relationships

Focusing on your relationships with others—and yourself—with gratitude can help pave the way to contentment. Contemplating these areas of your life can add focus to your journal entries too:

Treasured Friendships

Take a moment to honor and focus on your friends.

- Think about them one at a time—what they look like, how they smile and laugh, a key moment that you have shared together.

- If you were to move home or leave school/college/your job tomorrow, who would you want to contact to thank for the part they played in your life?

- Who would you like to leave a "legacy letter" for—to offer gratitude and encouragement for their future?

Finding Peace

Contentment comes from knowing that you have made peace with those to whom you caused pain, or that you have found a way to let go of past hurts and disappointments so that you can embrace your future with a thankful heart.

- Who have you fallen out of contact with, whom you still miss and remember from a time now past?

- If you are unable to reconnect with them or express your appreciation for their part in your life, what would you have liked to say to them in gratitude? Writing a letter, composing a verse, or creating something in gratitude can really help us to make peace with the past.

- Is there someone you need to let go of and forgive, in order to be free to live your life in a new way?

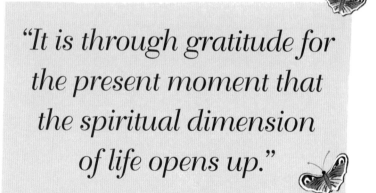

"It is through gratitude for the present moment that the spiritual dimension of life opens up."

Eckhart Tolle (1948–), author and spiritual teacher

Quiz: How Grateful is Your Attitude?

Try this quiz to get an overview of your approach to gratitude, and find out in which areas you could increase your gratitude or appreciation by noting which scores you got the most and reading the result on page 136.

1. I look forward to each new day:

No					*Sometimes*					*Yes*
0	1	2	3	4	5	6	7	8	9	10

2. I try to look for the positive in every situation:

No					*Sometimes*					*Yes*
0	1	2	3	4	5	6	7	8	9	10

3. I prefer to think the best of people:

No					*Sometimes*					*Yes*
0	1	2	3	4	5	6	7	8	9	10

4. I find it easy to offer help to others:

No					*Sometimes*					*Yes*
0	1	2	3	4	5	6	7	8	9	10

5. I find it easy to accept help from others:

No					Sometimes					Yes
0	1	2	3	4	5	6	7	8	9	10

6. I would help a stranger who was in need:

No					Sometimes					Yes
0	1	2	3	4	5	6	7	8	9	10

7. I often actively feel grateful for my friends and/or my family:

No					Sometimes					Yes
0	1	2	3	4	5	6	7	8	9	10

8. There is so much in the world that is beautiful and to be thankful for:

No					Sometimes					Yes
0	1	2	3	4	5	6	7	8	9	10

9. I own everything I need to be happy:

No					Sometimes					Yes
0	1	2	3	4	5	6	7	8	9	10

10. Generally in life, I feel very contented:

No					Sometimes					Yes
0	1	2	3	4	5	6	7	8	9	10

Any 0–3 scores
Sometimes in life we become so overwhelmed with our troubles that we feel stuck and alone. If any of your scores are on the lowside, please seek support from a friend or from a professional who could help you to shine a new light on your situation. There is much to feel grateful for in this evolving world of ours.

Mostly 4–6 scores
Do you live life with a touch of cynicism? Do you prioritize work over spending time with your friends and family? It is possible that you are shutting out companionship and support that could enrich your life and make you happier.

Mostly 7–10 scores
Feeling thankful comes easily to you. Did you score 10/10 on many of these questions? Your levels of gratitude will shore up your life with resilience and perseverance and help you to feel happier every day.

"Do not spoil what you have by desiring what you have not; remember that what you now have was once among the things you only hoped for."

Epicurus (341–270 BCE)

Conclusion: A Life of Gratitude

Conscious gratitude leads to contentment. Over time, it feeds the memory of a life well lived. When we are grateful for the beauty and variety of the world around us, we start to want to protect rather than destroy it. When we appreciate one another's differences, we start to celebrate those differences and welcome the contrast, rather than expecting everyone to be the same. When we stop regretting and start accepting, we start to live in a way that is more loving and realistic—and cast ourselves in a role where we cease to be victims of the past and start to make positive choices for the future. When we break the habit of negative self-talk and become grateful for who we are, we start to see the future more positively and enjoy our unique place in the world. When we are able to spot the reasons to be grateful in any situation, we step nearer to grace and to peace. Gratitude is, quite simply, the route to happiness. Make time to count your blessings—every day.

Resources

A selection of books, websites, videos, articles, and academic studies.

Inspiring Books And Videos

Schwartzberg, Louie, "Nature, Beauty, Gratitude," (featuring David Steindl-Rast), TED, 2011, www.ted.com/talks/louie_ schwartzberg_ nature_beauty_gratitude

Seligman, Martin E.P., *Learned Optimism: How to Change Your Mind and Your Life*, Vintage, 2006

Simon-Thomas, Emiliana R., "Compassion in the Brain," YouTube, September 25, 2013, www. youtube. com/watch?v=Ie4htPTeOvA

Soul Pancake, "An Experiment in Gratitude: The Science of Happiness," July 11, 2013, www. youtube.com/ watch?v=oHv6vTKD6lg

Steindl-Rast, David, "Want to Be Happy? Be Grateful," TED, 2013, www.ted.com/talks/david_ steindl_ rast_want_to_be_happy_be_grateful

Trice, Laura, "Remember to Say Thank You," TED, 2008, www.ted.com/ playlists/206/give_ thanks

Practical Resources And Websites

Exercises, questionnaires, and experiments in gratitude:

Authentic Happiness

The Penn State University website offers a range of questionnaires on gratitude, happiness, and other measures of well-being. You can take part too, by following this link: www.authentichappiness.sas.upenn.edu

The Franciscan Spiritual Center, "Musings on Gratitude"

www.fscaston.org/musings-on-gratitude

The Greater Good Science Center at the University of Berkeley

The University of Berkeley is at the forefront of current research into gratitude and its impact on our lives. Its website is a rich source of information: www.greatergood.berkeley.edu

The Happier Human

A generous-minded soul called Amit Amin has created the Happier Human website, a collection of personal musings and extensive resources: www.happierhuman.com

The Ripple Revolution

Curt Rosengren's Ripple Revolution website offers many routes to retuning our mindset to positive. This experiment is specifically focused on gratitude and is something any of us could do to great power and effect: www.ripplerevolution.com/would-this-gratitude- experiment-make-you-happier

David Steindl-Rast

www.gratefulness.org

Horatio's Garden

www.horatiosgarden.org.uk

Quilting resources

www.generations-quilt-patterns.com/quilt-guilds.html

www.quiltersguild.org.uk
www.quiltmuseum.org

Academic Studies

Many of these resources have been referred to during research for this book.

David DeSteno, Ye Li, Leah Dickens, and Jennifer S. Lerner, "Gratitude: A Tool for Reducing Economic Impatience," *Psychological Science* 25 (June 2014), 1262–67

Robert A. Emmons and M. E. McCullough, "Counting Blessings Versus Burdens: An Experimental Investigation of Gratitude and Subjective Well-being in Daily Life," *Journal of Personality and Social Psychology* 84/2 (2003), 377–89, www.psy.miami.edu/ faculty/ mmccullough/gratitude/Emmons_ McCullough_2003_JPSP.pdf

Robert A. Emmons and M. E. McCullough, "Highlights from the Research Project on Gratitude and Thankfulness: Dimensions and Perspectives of Gratitude," Universities of California, Davis, and Miami, 2003, www.psy.miami.edu/faculty/ mmccullough/Gratitude- Related%20 Stuff/highlights_fall_2003.pdf

"The Gratitude Questionnaire Six-item Form," www.psy.miami.edu/faculty/ mmccullough/ gratitude/GQ-6-scoring-interp.pdf, from Michael E. McCullough, Robert A. Emmons, and Jo-Ann Tsang, "The Grateful Disposition: A Conceptual and Empirical Topography," *Journal of Personality and Social Psychology*, 82/1 (2002), 112–27, available at www.greatergood. berkeley.edu/ pdfs/GratitudePDFs/7McCullough-GratefulDisposition.pdf

Laura E. Kurtz, and Sara B. Algoe, "Putting Laughter in Context: Shared Laughter as Behavioral Indicator of Relationship Well-being," *Personal Relationships* 22 (2015), 573–90, doi: 10.1111/pere.12095

Michael E. McCullough, Marcia B. Kimeldorf, and Adam D. Cohen, "An Adaptation for Altruism? The Social Causes, Social Effects, and Social Evolution of Gratitude," *Current Directions in Psychological Science* 17 (2008), 281–84, www. psy.miami. edu/faculty/mmccullough/Papers/Gratitude_CDPS_2008.pdf

Emily L. Polak and Michael E. McCullough, 'Is Gratitude an Alternative to Materialism?,' *Journal of Happiness Studies* 7 (2006), 343–60, www. psy.miami.edu/faculty/mmccullough/Papers/gratitude_materialism.pdf

Alexandra Sifferlin, "Why Being Thankful Is Good for You," *Time*, November 23, 2015, www.time.com/4124288/thanksgiving-day-2015- thankful-gratitude

University of North Carolina at Chapel Hill, "The Little Things: Gratitude and Shared Laughter Strengthen Romantic Partnerships," *Science Daily*, February 22, 2016, www.sciencedaily.com/releases/2016/02/160222144546.htm

Acknowledgments

With grateful thanks to the highly creative team at CICO—particularly Carmel Edmonds, for approaching me to write about such a fabulous subject, and for her skilled editing. This is as much Carmel's book as it is mine. Many thanks also to Kristine Pidkameny for commissioning the book. Thank you, too, to those who have shared their stories, provided feedback, or have contributed in some way, including: the Burges family, the Revd Canon Andrew Haviland, Sue Hook, Bev James, Libby Jones, Karen Kain, Sue Lanson, Mary Lou Nash, Vanda "Joy" North, Audrey Paisey, Revd Mary Ridgewell, Dr Christina Volkmann, and Pat Watson. And, of course, thank you to my wonderful family, especially my father and Richard.